This journal belongs to

_____

Growing in Grace

DEVOTIONAL
JOURNAL

BELLE CITY GIFTS

Published by Belle City Gifts™
Racine, Wisconsin, USA
www.bellecitygifts.com

Belle City Gifts is an imprint of BroadStreet Publishing Group, LLC
www.broadstreetpublishing.com

Growing in Grace Devotional Journal

© 2015 Laura Harris Smith

ISBN-13: 978-1-4245-4996-2 (hardcover)
ISBN-13: 978-1-4245-5035-7 (e-book)

Design by Chris Garborg | www.garborgdesign.com
Interior image by Jeorgi Smith | www.jeorgimages.com

Stock or custom editions of BroadStreet Publishing titles may be purchased in bulk for educational, business, ministry, fundraising, or sales promotional use. For information, please e-mail info@broadstreetpublishing.com.

Printed in China

GROWING IN...

Introduction

What do you see when you look around at God's creation? I see growth. Everything made with human hands decays, but all that God makes flourishes and multiplies. Growth is God's idea! The Scriptures encourage us to "grow in the grace and knowledge of our Lord and Savior Jesus Christ" (2 Peter 3:18 ESV). That's what this devotional journal is designed to do for you.

Each topic has been prayerfully chosen to address the myriad of maladies your heart encounters on a regular basis, and the poems are their medicine. I'm not aware of another book like this, and I trust these devotional poems will be both thought provoking and entertaining.

As a poet of hundreds of poems, I am genuinely proud of this inspirational collection, from A to Z. Some were written during very dark nights of the soul for me, and rereading them makes me want to reassure the woman writing them that not only will she make it through, but that the words she is tearfully scribbling will one day bless thousands of people. What a testament of God's redemption! Remember God's unfailing love as you grow in creativity, joy, persistence, virtue, and much more—recording your journey on these beautiful pages.

If this content inspires your own writing, please see the About the Author page at the back of the journal. I offer online writing classes where poetry is one of the many writing genres covered. At the back I've also included the rhyme schemes of each poem so that you can begin your own poetic education.

As you turn each of the following pages, my prayer for you is that you receive daily from His fullness, "grace upon grace" (John 1:16 ESV).

Enjoy!

Laura Harris Smith

Affirmation

It really is so simple
It's not a new ideal
The people that I love deserve to know just how I feel!

My words that cheer do matter
My pep talks are first aid
They give support to boost the sick, the sad and underpaid

But what if I withhold them?
What if I never share?
Will anyone else be to blame if folks think I don't care?

My friends await my praises
They crave my accolades
They need to know I'm here for them; they need to know I've prayed

My family is my ministry
Affirming them is key
For if I don't they maybe won't know how to champion me

God, give me words to wow them
Please let me be Your voice
I might just be the last small cheer before their next big choice

This saying is faithful, and concerning these things
I desire that you affirm confidently.

TITUS 3:8 WEB

I can start by disciplining myself more. Look for affirmation of God's love way He is with us.
Help family know that He is with us.
Look in the Bible for affirmations
LK-14:11
1 Cor 1 4-6
2 Thes 1:3 Work on joy for it leads to keysing your faith in God.

GROWING IN...

Boldness

My thoughts have been so scattered; my mind has been so tossed
And in the wind's opinion, my nerve is easily lost

I want to be more bold, God; I want the lion's roar
I want to find the bravery that ends this inner war

I fix my eyes on You, Lord; I trust You, come what may
And once the winds are listening, You'll tell me what to say

The righteous are as bold as a lion.

PROVERBS 28:1 NIV

Would others describe you as bold? Why or why not?

GROWING IN...

Charity

While in another city once
with Christmas just in view
I met a man with cup in hand
whose coat was torn in two

He needed help; he needed hope
He needed food and drink
And as I gave him all I had
it gave me pause to think

I told this man of Someone past
Who'd helped me one time too
Who gave to me all that He had
to make my life brand new

He held my hand and as I spoke
His eyes filled up with tears
He acted like the hug I gave
had been his first in years

I left that town, turned upside down
inside my thankful heart
A homeless soul had found a home
Received a brand new start

With all His homes in heav'n and earth
Christ searches for one more
The irony: we hold the key
that lets Him in the door

And above all these things put on charity, which is the bond of perfectness.

COLOSSIANS 3:14 KJV

When was the last time you were charitable to a stranger,
and how can you show charity this week?

Commitment

I don't know what I ever did to win the love you give
But without what I've grown to know I surely could not live

You fill up all my senses when you touch my face, my skin
And love the me I am today despite the me I've been

This frame would never know the way to any other arms
Nor could it be beguiled away with imitation charms

No other love could breathe with mine and blow the past away
and whisper vows that serve as wind for sails we raise today

No other touch could take me back and make me young once more
No other face could age with mine; no other face but yours

No other voice can pierce my pride and promptly calm me down
or lift me up when other voices drive me to the ground

No other heart could win me; none other could keep time
Nor could another pair of feet dance through our uphill climb

I pray for future memories; I pray for them today
I pray we make them one by one and that they come to stay

My mind will always find you; it knows you are its home
It can't get lost or lose its way wherever it may roam

My yesterdays are in you, they see me through today
You'll carry my tomorrows, no matter what they weigh

It's simple yet astounding; no doubt all by design
I'm here because you'll have me; you're here because you're mine

You will honor God through this genuine act of service because of your commitment.

2 CORINTHIANS 9:13 GW

Who have you made commitments to in your life,
and how can you honor those commitments more?

Consecration

I stare into the endless blue
giving all I am to You
unsure of my path, unsure of what's true
denying myself and trusting Your view

I've crucified dreams and brushed them aside
knowing they're dead 'til they match Your stride
confused and alone, in Your arms I will hide
You are my Maker and I am Your bride

God, You see fully what I'll one day be
You've covered my eyes so I'll trust You to see
Relying on You, it's here I am free
Forever I'll stay consecrated to Thee

*Consecrate yourselves, for tomorrow the LORD
will do amazing things among you.*

JOSHUA 3:5 NIV

What does it mean to be consecrated, and how can you more deeply demonstrate your consecration to God this week?

Contentment

Time to confess
I'm really a mess
and I know what's the root of it all
These feelings arise
and tell me great lies
at the bank, at my job or the mall

They tell me I'm late
overdraft, overweight
and that I will never advance
They make me believe
I have less than I need
of things and rings and romance

To live satisfied
is hopeless (I've tried)
in a world that is screaming for more
The minute you're pleased
you're suddenly teased
with the next big thing next door

But what if I dared
to not be compared
to a person a place or a thing?
And what if I chose
when those feelings arose
to be happy, content and then sing?

I might be surprised
at the peace in their eyes
when I do not react to their flaunt
And my Shepherd's supply
will never run dry
and because of Him I shall not want

But godliness with contentment is great gain.

1 TIMOTHY 6:6 NIV

Are you content? How can you grow in contentment this week?

_____

_____

_____

_____

_____

_____

_____

_____

_____

_____

_____

_____

Courtesy

Whatever happened to being polite,
well-mannered and pleasant and kind?
And why do we disregard life's dearest gestures
and hurriedly leave them behind?

We used to say "yes ma'am" and "no sir" and "thank you"
and ask God to bless every sneeze
But now we're more bridled, we feel more entitled
and barely can muster a "please"

Stop your critiquing, please look at who's speaking
and lay down your phone for a while
Do not interrupt or be rudely abrupt; watch your tone
and for heaven's sake, smile!

Don't be so driven, shake a hand if it's given,
and please use said hand if you yawn
Take your neighbor a meal, ask his wife how she feels
and then when they're gone mow their lawn

And when on the road, save the rage, don't explode;
when parking, be kind, have a heart
Let someone cut line, change a tire, pay a fine
and take back that stray shopping cart

Hold a door, feed the poor, take your friend to the store,
go above and beyond for your brother
And when on the bus and a baby does fuss
give your seat to that tired nursing mother

Remember my friend, don't ever drop in,
call first then go ready to serve
Serve at church, while you're at it, don't be too dogmatic
and stay off your pastor's last nerve

Say "you're welcome" when thanked, and sorry, when spanked
and know when to keep your lip zipped
Be on time when you dine, grab the tab as you gab,
and don't jilt your waitress her tip

If we'd keep in mind to be gracious and kind
and when not, to make speedy amends
We'd never again bring grief to our kin
or find ourselves lacking in friends

Show perfect courtesy toward all people.

TITUS 3:1–2 ESV

Would others describe you as courteous?
Who do you need to offer your help to this week as an act of thoughtfulness?

Creativity

Maybe you think
you're on the brink
of the next big innovation
Or maybe you are
left-brainy, by far
and prefer administration

Both of these breeds
with all of their deeds
reflect the Father's flair
So we only cause trouble
when we live in our bubble
and constantly try to compare

We each have a piece
of the constant release
of the creative Creator's heart
Whether dancing and painting
and entertaining
or the Administrative Arts

One thing is for sure
the entrepreneur
requires both to win
And I'm never late
when I'm asked to create
if I let the Creator in

Thou sendest forth Thy spirit, they are created:
and Thou renewest the face of the earth.

PSALM 104:30 KJV

Would you call yourself creative? If you are God's child and He is the Creator, then how can you show your creativity regularly in your own way?

Deliverance

Rescue me, oh great God, and set me free
Liberate my captive heart of its chains
You are the only One who has its key
I am the only one who feels its pains
At birth my heart was whole, my spirit too
But one by one the tribulations came
And on their heels came grief before I knew
Then I was left with bitterness and blame
You've saved my spirit; now please save my mind
Erase the fears the years have nursed and fed
Repair the built-in trust that's been maligned
Replace it with salvation in its stead
There are no tactics left to see me through
Deliverance can only come from You

I wait for Your deliverance, O LORD.

GENESIS 49:18 NET

In what areas of your life do you need deliverance,
and from what or whom?

_____

_____

_____

_____

_____

_____

_____

_____

_____

_____

_____

_____

_____

_____

_____

_____

_____

Dependence

His will His bill
I like pickles, only dill
But I'm such an imbecile
When I'm stressed and need to chill
On my patio's a grill
Where we eat our daily kill
Next to yellow daffodils
And a passing whippoorwill

Still...

It really makes me ill
when I break into a shrill
'cause the day has been uphill
and my promise ain't fulfilled!
So I find my trusty quill
And my ink (which usually spills)
and I write and write until
I am much less volatile

Fill...

My life with just Your will
Not my excess; not my frill
Take my scum and all my skill
and cook it as Your daily kill
Take what's left and please instill
All Your holy chlorophyll
'Til Your sweet aroma spills
from Leningrad to Louisville
Oh thrill!

I was dependent on You from birth;
from my mother's womb You have been my God.

PSALM 22:10 ISV

Describe what is happening in your life that is creating greater dependency upon God and how you are responding to Him.

_____

_____

_____

_____

_____

_____

_____

_____

_____

_____

_____

_____

_____

_____

_____

_____

Discernment

I saw you at the altar; I heard the prayer you prayed
I made good notes and plotted, our next game of charades

I thrive on your warm welcome, your swift and sure embrace
I spread from there quite quickly; my aim is for your face

I'm lurking in the church halls or at a passing door
I'm at your next staff meeting or on the nursery floor

I'm in that random e-mail or phone call that comes in
with news that doesn't please you; injustice is my friend

I know you don't deserve me; it's such a crying shame
I'll always dodge the credit; I have so many names

I detonate on impact; I'm Satan's hand grenade
I want to take your brotherhood if you'll just make the trade

I'm where you least expect me; I watch for all the signs
And in I come when you've been wronged to comfort you each time

You're right and they are wrong; just make your mind up now
A breach is just a breath away; division is my vow

Let's you and I birth grudges; let's make their words unclear
Don't worry what to say now; I'll whisper in your ear

I need for you to hold me; oh please be deaf and dumb
Forgiveness isn't stylish, or shown where I come from

I'm not a nasty rumor; I'm not a hidden sin
I'll gladly become both though, if you'll just let me in

I'm not a mere annoyance; I'm not your common sense
I'm never on your radar; I am your next offense

Teach me good judgment and discernment, for I rely on Your commands.
PSALM 119:66 HCSB

In what areas have you become offended and not discerned that a spirit of offense was influencing you? Which relationships in your life do you discern require extra attention right now if they are to survive and thrive?

_____

_____

_____

_____

_____

_____

_____

_____

_____

_____

_____

_____

_____

_____

Discipline

I need to be more disciplined
I need a new routine
My flesh, though, is not interested
in what that just might mean

I'm quick to set a regimen
But slow at self-control
I wish there was a medicine
to help me meet my goal

If order's in my schedule, though
my flesh will learn the drill
And if I'll bridle whims and grow
my heart will train my will

*For the moment all discipline seems painful rather than pleasant,
but later it yields the peaceful fruit of righteousness to those
who have been trained by it.*

HEBREWS 12:10–11 NLT

Better than anyone else, you know the areas of your life that need discipline. What are they?

GROWING IN...

Discretion

Above the chin, beneath the eyes
There the vile volcano lies

Spewing toxic undertones
Murder with a megaphone

Cast your lots to dabble on
Mumble, mutter, babble on

Mountains made from small faux pas
"Blah, blah, blah, blah, blah, blah, blahs"

Whisper, chatter, gush, and spout
Poison and malignant doubt

Venom verified by hate
Greedy for a double-date

Guard the gap and close the spout
Let no deadly thing come out

Lest I wake in the abyss
Prisoner to its crafty kiss

The discretion of a man makes him slow to anger.
It is his glory to overlook an offense.

PROVERBS 19:11 WEB

In what ways do you need to be more discreet, cautious, and guarded in your speech and conversations with others?

Endurance

You can't tie your shoes 'til you lace them
You can't eat your chips with a fork
You can't make your bed
if you're under the spread
And you can't put much stock in the stork

Your countenance won't change with a face lift
And you won't reason well if you stare
You can't move big mountains
with impressive big fountains
if they flow from your eyes without prayer

See, you can't judge a race at the start line
And you can't call it quits 'til it's done
And you can't run a mile
then fall down in a pile
'cause it seems you're behind everyone

It takes faith to tie shoes or move mountains
Even with it, some days just ain't fun
But you won't win big races
without faith or tied laces
so get up and thank God you can run!

*For you need endurance, so that after you have done God's will,
you may receive what was promised.*

HEBREWS 10:36 HCSB

In what areas do you want to grow in endurance so that God can perfectly work out what He has promised you?

Excellence

I long to give my best to life each day
and life itself longs not to live halfway

A perfect life is not what God requires
but fine-tuned faith, perfected through life's fires

Each job I do should hone my talents more
improving me, compelling me to soar

Lord, let me beget caliber each day
unparalleled, with excellence, I pray

*Now, my daughter, do not fear. I will do for you whatever you ask,
for all my people in the city know that you are a woman of excellence.*

RUTH 3:11 NASB

What things come to mind that you have been doing only halfway, and how can you do them with more excellence?

Faith

Whenever I have questions
whenever I'm in doubt
I think of all you've stood through
and those thoughts lead me out

I celebrate your faith now
I marvel at your hope
You need to know it strengthens
so many trying to cope

God cheered you when you conquered
He held you when you cried
And I was right there watching
You never broke your stride

Your confident reliance
is hard earned, not naïve
God knows this world is different
because you have believed

*Now faith is the substance of things hoped for,
the evidence of things not seen.*

HEBREWS 11:1 KJV

In what areas of your life do you have the greatest faith,
and which areas do you desire to grow in faith?

Fearlessness

Everyone who knows you well can see it plain as day
the way you walk right to the edge and leap without delay

You're not unwise, you weigh the cost, but still, you take your chances
and always listen to your heart despite the circumstances

The pioneering way you live is pure, secure, and bold
Your courage is heroic, your battle scars are gold

So if no one has told you, if you yourself can't see
your stalwart heart has freed you, and me, to some degree

Keep leading and keep loving, march forward, resolute
but glance back and be strengthened by the fans you will recruit

*Your fearlessness will be to them a sure token of impending
destruction, but to you it will be a sure token of your
salvation—a token coming from God.*

PHILIPPIANS 1:28 WEY

In what areas do you want to move forward boldly,
even though you may be afraid right now?

GROWING IN...

Flexibility

The seaside tree
will surely see
great tempests without end
But stronger so
when hard winds blow
is the tree that learns to bend

It does not mean
its roots are weak
nor that its stance is vague
It simply proves
the sap that moves
throughout its humble veins

*I'm flexible, adaptable, and able to do and be whatever is needed
for all kinds of people so that in the end I can use every means
at my disposal to offer them salvation.*

1 CORINTHIANS 9:22 VOICE

I prefer a flexible heart to an inflexible ritual.

MATTHEW 12:7 MSG

Would you call yourself flexible or inflexible? What are three ways you can be less rigid in your relationships, including in your relationship with God?

Forgiveness

It feels like a good rubdown when you've failed and done your worst
It seems a noble option, 'til you're asked to give it first

It tastes like milk and honey when it's offered down to you
Yet smells to the high heavens when you didn't get your due

It sounds like angels singing when it's offered and received
Yet when we won't extend it, bitterness is conceived

It doesn't search for justice or agree to disagree
It cuts the flesh, reveals the heart, releases destiny

*And whenever you make a prayer, let there be forgiveness in your hearts,
if you have anything against anyone; so that you may have forgiveness for
your sins from your Father who is in heaven.*

MARK 11:25 BBE

Who is the Lord showing you that you need to forgive,
so that you yourself might be forgiven?

Friendship

Today I was thinking about you and me
and wondered without you just where I would be
without all your phone calls, without every smile
without your encouragements in every trial

I tried to imagine you not by my side
each time that I cheered; each time that I cried
What if we'd not spoken that first time we met?
What if when we're older we somehow forget?

I think all my thinking won't get me too far
Let's just say I'm me because you're who you are

I was in the ripeness of my days,
when the friendship of God was in my tent.

JOB 29:4 RSV

What do you look for in a good friend,
and what kind of friend would your friends say you are?

Generosity

If giving is a virtue
And charity converts you
Then shouldn't every need be met by now?
But if your heart desserts you
And all your wealth perverts you
So that you donate just to take a bow
Then pity might avert you
(Not overly exert you)
So that you never learn how to endow
But if the hurting hurt you
And sympathy reverts you
Benevolence will come, my friend, and how

*You will be enriched in every way so that you can be generous
on every occasion, and through us your generosity will result
in thanksgiving to God.*

2 CORINTHIANS 9:11 NIV

Name a time when someone was generous to you.
What are some ways you can show generosity this week?

_____

_____

_____

_____

_____

_____

_____

_____

_____

_____

_____

_____

_____

_____

_____

_____

_____

_____

Gentleness

Like the gentle breeze
The tender, tenor winds sing
And harmony comes

Words now flow with ease
Hard hearts melt with sunny spring
Winter leaves unsung

A clement reprise
Love is what the genteel bring
Life is in their tongue

Let your gentleness be evident to all. The Lord is near.

PHILIPPIANS 4:5 NIV

A gentle answer turns away wrath, but a harsh word stirs up anger.

PROVERBS 15:1 NIVUK

Thinking of the most gentle person in your life as a role model, what are some ways you can exhibit gentleness this week?

_____

_____

_____

_____

_____

_____

_____

_____

_____

_____

_____

_____

_____

_____

_____

_____

_____

_____

GROWING IN...

Gratitude

If every day I filled my mouth with gratitude and thanks
And let appreciation bridge the gaps and fill the blanks

The vain nonrecognition of the blessings that are mine
Most surely seems so petty when I grumble, gripe and whine

I'd cause myself less trouble and I'd spare my heart some aches
If I would count my blessings and stop numbering mistakes

To live like I'm indebted, to God and those I love
Would bring me double blessings that I'd be more worthy of

*Therefore, since we receive a kingdom which cannot be shaken,
let us show gratitude, by which we may offer to God an acceptable
service with reverence and awe.*

HEBREWS 12:28 NASB

Today, repent of ingratitude.
What things in your life do you have to be grateful for?

_____

_____

_____

_____

_____

_____

_____

_____

_____

_____

_____

_____

_____

_____

_____

_____

_____

_____

_____

_____

_____

Health

I need to be in health, Lord
This road has been so long
It's been a good few years, God
But today I'm not so strong

It was another hard one
My head wants to explode
Along with my broad shoulders
It carries quite a load

My health is in Your hands, God
I have great peace of mind
But in this unhealed body
That peace remains confined

*Beloved, I pray that in all respects you may prosper
and be in good health, just as your soul prospers.*

3 JOHN 2 NASB

Peace of mind means a healthy body.

PROVERBS 14:30 NCV

Are there sicknesses you are dealing with in your body?
List them, giving each one to the Great Physician in exchange for His healing.

Honor

Honor is a way of life, a state of mind, a view
Despite if you are showing it or it's been shown to you

It's giving adulation to that teacher in your life
It's valuing your husband or deferring to your wife

It's honoring your parents; a commandment with a vow
that you will live a long and happy life, beginning now

It's venerating clergy; taking time to ease their strain
Saluting every soldier; paying homage to the slain

If accolades were silver and respect was bars of gold
We'd stuff our pockets full of both and never dare withhold

But honor isn't just esteem we know we should be giving
It's honest, brave integrity that infiltrates our living

It's holding fast to principles and goodness at all cost
It's guarding reputation so no character is lost

A good name is worth riches and a bad one breaks the bank
So live your life uprightly and it's honor that you'll thank

The wise will inherit honor, but fools get disgrace.

PROVERBS 3:35 ESV

New honors will come to me continually, and I will always have great strength.

JOB 29:20 NIV

Who in your life does God want you to honor,
and how will you demonstrate that this week?

Hope

Feeling my way along the walls
hoping that this will be
the very last corner I have to crawl
pretending that I can see

How did I get here on the ground
when before I was standing firm?
Somehow I fell down, and now I resound
of another humbling term

It's dark in this place where no eye can see
where hope is the sole ray that beams
But some say that hope in faith's recipe
Wakes the substance of all things yet seen

This room is much larger than at my first glance
when I first launched the search for the light
And somehow my senses have all been enhanced
as I've walked all this way without sight

Still I know the day nears when the lights will come on
Heaven's wiring has destined my hand
to map out this room 'til the walls are all gone
and enlighten those left where I stand

It's dark in this place where no eye can see
where hope is the sole ray that beams
But some say that hope in faith's recipe
Wakes the substance of all things yet seen

May the God of hope fill you with all joy and peace as you trust in him,
so that you may overflow with hope by the power of the Holy Spirit.

ROMANS 15:13 NIV

Who in your life needs hope right now? Despite your own areas of despair,
list some ways you can be the answer to someone else's hopelessness
while you trust God to work out your own situation.

Humility

God, are You humble? Or are You like me?
Forgive me for asking, but I'm curious, You see
'Cause I couldn't do all that You've done and be
So patient when no one is thankful

If I'd created color, and painted the sky
Formed the first baby, brought it forth, heard it cry
If the universe needed my word to survive
Would I maybe be a little hard to live with?

I try to be humble 'cause You say I should be
But I really don't want to (now there is the key!)
'Cause I think I'm afraid that no one will see me
When... isn't that what You're after in the first place?

But why? You're the One who decided my form
Then gave me these dreams that are far from the norm
Lord, why did You make me then make me transform
Into an image that is so out of reach?

How can I live here, January through September
and mirror You there, just a spark, just an ember?
I know You live in Me, but I'm human, remember?
And aren't You the One who decided to make me this way?

What a comfort to know that I'm made in Your image
That the road I am on proves I'm part of Your lineage
Wrestling hard to stay low; it's a death; it's a privilege
For He who humbled Himself was obedient even unto death

Even with revelation that none came before You
Knowing no man or beast can succeed and ignore You
I find myself wanting to do great feats for You
Instead of just letting You work through me

So if I die to self, I will look more like You?
Resurrected for victory in all I pursue?
Invisible to enemies, out of reach, out of view!
Okay then Lord, help me to see humility as Your gift to me today

Yes, all of you be submissive to one another, and be clothed with humility, for
"God resists the proud, But gives grace to the humble."
1 PETER 5:5 NKJV

What are the areas of your life that you could be tempted
to become prideful about? Journal a prayer to God surrendering
those people, places, and things to Him.

Identity

Go find your personality
then claim originality
and individuality
and let nobody deceive you

Conform not to the world nearby
Nobody has your laugh, your cry
Be who you are and don't comply
to the image of who you're not

Your selfhood rests in God's design
You're not from some production line
So you can't mope and moan and pine
wishing you were somebody else

Unique, distinct, so prized and loved
You'll stand up tall, a head above
When you get revelation of
the fact that you're one of a kind!

Once you had no identity as a people; now you are God's people.

1 PETER 2:10 NLT

What are the unique traits you have that make you, you?
Thank God for them one by one!

GROWING IN...

Influence

All influence and impact
is given from above
Some use it for their pleasure
I use it to show love

I pray that you will know that love
and that you'll stop and pray
and ask Christ to come in your heart
He is the only way

I never want to push you
but when I pray I hear
God saying that He loves you
and wants to hold you near

We need much more than teachings
We need love that's alive
God sent His Son to love the world
And for the world, He died

But death could not constrain Him
In Him there was no sin
Christ's love for us was so strong
It made Him live again

We too can live forever
By asking for His love
By praying just one prayer to Him
He fills us from above

I do want to influence you
I don't want to offend
But I just had to tell you
God loves you, my dear friend

You must influence them; do not let them influence you!

JEREMIAH 15:19 NLT

Who are the people in your life under your influence?
And how are you using that influence?

GROWING IN...

Intimacy

I know You as a king and as a judge
I know You as a savior and a lord
But when You stop and give my heart a nudge
there's something more that cannot be ignored
It's here You want to sit with me as friend
discuss the day and ask me how I feel
My deepest inner thoughts You apprehend
if I will only take the time to kneel
The friends who claim to love me come and go
They spout forth great affinities and praise
But You're the only friend I can't outgrow
And You're the only one who ever stays
Familiar, faithful friend, who does cajole
The champion of companions heals my soul

No prophet ever rose again in Israel like Moses,
whom the LORD knew with such great intimacy.

Deuteronomy 34:10 ISV

In what relationships is intimacy difficult for you (with God or others)? Ask God to show you why and to give you His grace to grow in intimacy.

Joy

Happiness is just a phase
It's great delight with great delays
But when joy comes it comes and stays forever

It fills your face with utter glee
trades fears for pure felicity
and makes you shout with jubilee each day

Though hard times come, true joy remains
It pays no mind to strife and strains
It even helps with labor pains, I've found

It triumphs when the funds are low
It never sinks or worse, plateaus
It always gives and somehow grows much stronger

Don't be dejected and sad, for the joy of the LORD is your strength!

NEHEMIAH 8:10 NLT

What things bring you the most joy?
In what areas does God want to bring you greater joy?

Kindness

Kindness is a dying art
although I'm not sure why
But let us look inside your heart
then you give your reply

When is the last time in your life
you helped a friend all day?
Or recognized a stranger's strife
and for their meal did pay?

Or showed some hospitality
and opened up your home
Displayed congeniality
for travelers on the roam?

Delivered meals, imparted grace
or washed your neighbor's car?
Drove friends to kingdom come and back?
(or some place less bizarre)

Such altruism can survive
When we decide to share
Kindheartedness is still alive
Each time we show we care

Happy [are] the kind—because they shall find kindness.

MATTHEW 5:7 YLT

When was the last time you went out of your way to be kind, and to whom?
Who is God leading you to be kind to today, and what will you do?

_____

_____

_____

_____

_____

_____

_____

_____

_____

_____

_____

_____

_____

_____

_____

_____

_____

_____

_____

GROWING IN...

Leadership

Take false caution out of me
Fill me with transparency

Clean my heart, my home, my hands
as my leadership expands

Govern, guide, and promise me
strict accountability

Test me, try my wherewithal
or don't let me lead at all

*If God has given you leadership ability,
take the responsibility seriously.*

Romans 12:8 NLT

Who are you leading? To where are you leading them?
How do you want to lead them better?

GROWING IN...

Love

I loved you on the pathway we traveled long ago
I loved the way the sun shone in rain or sleet or snow

I loved the trails we traipsed on and interstates of gold
I loved the roads we raced on and sidewalks where we strolled

I loved you on the highway when crowded lanes got fast
I loved you at the exit ramp when we did wave our last

I loved you on the turnpike although it was cut short
I loved you on the dirt road, I loved you at the fork

I loved you going uphill, I loved you down the lane
I loved you at the U-turn, there's no need to explain

I loved you on the freeway that wasn't free at all
I'm sorry that it cost you, I'm here to pay your toll

I'll love you when you're poor or even when you're rich
I'll love you when you're moving, I'll love you in the ditch

No roadblock is too fearsome, no alley is too dark
No detour is too distant, no matter where you park

The avenue is clear now, washed by the tears you've cried
I'm with you on your journey, each step, each stomp and stride

I'll love you near the waters, I'll love you in the sky
I'll love you come what may on earth and in the by and by

By this all will know that you are My disciples, if you have love for one another.

JOHN 13:35 NKJV

Describe the kind of love you desire to express with others in your life.

Loyalty

Constant, steady
Lifelong friend
Iron-like love that knows no end

Sure, authentic
tried and true
faithful, firm, unfailing you

The longest road
the farthest star
you always say is not too far

Of all the things
I'm most sure of
where'er I go, I'll find your love

Many a man proclaims his own loyalty,
but who can find a trustworthy man?

PROVERBS 20:6 HCSB

Who are the most loyal people in your life?
How do you demonstrate loyalty in your relationships?

Maturity

There once was a girl, so mature
Responsible, wise, and secure
'Til she opened her mouth
And the chitchat went south
And then no one was so sure!

Grow to maturity.

2 CORINTHIANS 13:11 NLT

Therefore let us move beyond the elementary teachings about Christ and be taken forward to maturity, not laying again the foundation of repentance from acts that lead to death, and of faith in God.

HEBREWS 6:1 NIV

What attributes in your character need to mature,
and what is one specific way you can grow in each of these areas?

_____

_____

_____

_____

_____

_____

_____

_____

_____

_____

_____

_____

_____

_____

_____

_____

_____

_____

Mercy

I wondered if I might, at first
write down my thoughts in rhyme and verse
To find the good this pain has brought
But truth be told, I'm overwrought

I can't pretend a lesson's learned
when all I see are bridges burned
I do not understand God's ways
on this or any other day

He lets me hurt, He bids me pray
but lets you turn and walk away
I hate to say it but it's true:
I need to see Him chasten you

I want fair play, I want it now
I want my day in court, and how
For if it all was read aloud
my case would surely sway the crowd

See, justice is my closest kin
but you need mercy now, my friend
You've set your heart high on a shelf
But in the end, you've hurt yourself

You closed a door and locked it tight
I've knocked and knocked with all my might
I need to turn and walk away
But this last thing I need to say

I would've loved, I would've stood
I would've brought you all things good
I could've served; I could defend
I could've been your perfect friend

I fear for you when no one's left
when you're alone, afraid, bereft
I wonder who'll run to your side
from all those whom you once denied

You'll see your fears were nothing more
than something to be sorry for
And maybe then I'll get to say
the words I am denied today

Mercy triumphs over judgment. JAMES 2:13 ESV

Who are the people who have hurt you the most recently,
and list some reasons why they need to be shown mercy?

_____

_____

_____

_____

_____

_____

_____

_____

_____

_____

_____

_____

Nutrition

I'd like to give you food for thought if you'll give me permission
and possibly it could offend (I have a keen suspicion)
But these few words might wake you up and set you on a mission
since helping you live long and strong is purely my ambition
It's time you take back your physique and give it definition
Stop pigging out, start working out and lose your inhibition
Start walking, running, stepping, and do body demolition
Stop acting like those long lost curves are just an apparition

Get serious about your chow and call a dietician
or someone who can take your fork and give an admonition
Then count your carbs and calories as if you're a tactician
and chew your food well as you eat and take an intermission!
Take vitamins and supplements and contact your physician
especially if underweight and suffering malnutrition
Start viewing food as medicine and snacks as ammunition
Take back your bod and whip it into absolute submission

It's possible to get a plan and make a smart transition
It starts with just awareness and an honest, frank admission
Then tell your friends and family and make some new traditions
Then watch your whole anatomy receive a recondition
The time is now for you to give your Maker recognition
He crafted you one of a kind, a limited edition
So start today with hope and claim your sunny disposition
It's waiting for you on the other side of good nutrition

And God said, "Behold, I have given you every plant yielding seed that is on the face of all the earth, and every tree with seed in its fruit. You shall have them for food."

GENESIS 1:29 ESV

Or do you not know that your body is a temple of the Holy Spirit within you, whom you have from God? You are not your own, for you were bought with a price. So glorify God in your body.

1 CORINTHIANS 6:19–20 KJV

Name three unhealthy foods you need to remove entirely
from your diet, and three healthy foods you need to add.
Ask God for the grace to grow in this area of change.

Obedience

My mind's at war with duty
It wants to not comply
I tell it not to argue
It only questions why

If I rely on strength alone
the future seems so bleak
My spirit is so willing
but my flesh is still so weak

My heart defers to You, God
conforming to Your Word
It tethers me consistently
to vows You've overheard

Convict my wandering feet, Lord
and teach them to obey
So that I hear You call me
and run without delay

Certainly, obedience is better than sacrifice.

1 SAMUEL 15:22 NET

Delayed obedience is disobedience. What areas
of your walk with God need immediate repentance and attention?

Patience

Slow and steady wins the race
but can't we please pick up the pace?

It seems we're always pushing through
and answers seem long overdue

The world is moving, rushing by
and patience is in short supply

But when I stop within the crowd
I see the peace you live out loud

You say life comes, as too does death
You're never fazed or out of breath

You know the long run turns into
the surest path that gets us through

In your patience possess ye your souls.

LUKE 21:19 KJV

Would you call yourself a patient person? Names the areas of your life that have required patience and what it has accomplished in you.

Peace

Into a boat, and then out to sea
they followed You toward Galilee
They went, unsure of where they were going
They were just watching You, 'til the wind started blowing

Then shifting their focus and changing their gaze
their eyes were soon fixed on the wind and the waves
Why is it perspective is so hard to keep?
And why, when I'm drowning, do You seem so asleep?

You slept in the boat as the waves formed great walls
while they panicked, You dreamed and envisioned their calls
And the Galilee Sea, with it's undisturbed form
gave up its peace, and gave way to storm

Its waters are shallow and still on all sides
only twelve miles long, and a mere seven wide
So how do such waves burst out of such peace
to record the worst storms in the whole Middle East?

With the Great Mediterranean just fifty miles west
and Lebanon's mountains fifty miles east, at best
The Sea of Galilee is nestled in between
and although it is typically still and serene

One low-pressure system coming from the Great Sea
crashes into those hills, then back to Galilee
And suddenly, its waters are stirred and transformed
and from perfect peace comes a violent storm

Oh God, will it ever be different in me
with these mountains I can't seem to cast to the sea?
Can You teach me to see them and not see their size
looking at them with faith and not with my eyes?

You're the God of all flesh and that includes me
Can You speak to my mind like You spoke to the sea?
Since faith is the substance of those things not seen
I must walk by faith, not by sight, in between

And though storms rage near me, they won't rage within
I'll "be of good cheer" choosing joy to the end!
I will walk by my faith; I will walk on the sea
I won't follow signs but they will follow me

And on that great day when my faith will be sight
the faith of those watching will reach a new height
Calm my faith, calm my heart, calm the wind and waves too
As I bide in this boat, full at rest next to You

Now the Lord of peace Himself give you peace always by all means.
The Lord be with you all. 2 THESSALONIANS 3:16 NKJV

On a scale of one to ten, how much peace do you walk in on a day-to-day
basis? What would help you be more at peace, resting in the Lord?

_____

_____

_____

_____

_____

_____

_____

GROWING IN...

Perseverance

I've got a problem, maybe you have the same
Mine searches me out and it knows me by name
Its goal is to use me and leave me ashamed
to kill, steal and destroy

It met no resistance, once upon a time
For years I allowed it; for years I was blind
And then I awoke and saw what was mine
although I have still yet to hold it

I've asked believing; I've fasted; I've prayed
I've heard God's instruction and learned to obey
I've seen others get what I want in one day
and learned to love without envy

I've spoken to mountains; I've named and I've claimed
I've bound and I've loosed and had things stay the same
I've warred with the name that's above all names
while it seemed to profit me nothing

Through visions and dreams my instruction's been sealed
hearing more than can ever be shared or revealed
staying quiet so God's secret plans are concealed
and released then at just the right moment

I've trusted, rested, hoped for and doubted
I've ached with self-pity, I've grieved and I've pouted
I've seen power come when I've whispered or shouted
for I've learned it's not your volume, but your authority

88

I've seen my protection in prayer as I kneeled
I've seen with my eyes His great buckler and shield
discovering wholeness as you wait to be healed
and I have dwelled in the shelter of the Most High

I've drank from a fountain, in gulps and in sips
I've seen the Son shine in a total eclipse
I've tasted sweet praise pouring over bruised lips
and I've felt Him inhabit that praise

Hungry for more, I've tasted some power
I've drank from a cup that is sweet and still sour
I've starved my flesh hoping to feast at some hour
only to feast once again on the fruit of patience

I've swam upstream in water that's muddy
I've knocked and I've knocked 'til my knuckles are bloody
I've heard people say without words that I'm nutty
and can honestly say I've died to all reputation

Blessed is he who can't see, yet believes
Perhaps it's an office we all should achieve
The price though, is more than we ever perceive
when we start praying those dangerous prayers for patience

Does faith say this is the day, if it's not?
Can God stretch a scene if He's building a plot?
Do you judge those who wait or want what they've got?
Knowing that it's through faith and patience we receive God's promises

We can't live without it; we can barely live through it
It's a fruit of God's Spirit and there's no shortcuts to it
If you find one it only reveals that you blew it
'cause King James said it best when He called it "longsuffering"

Are you willing to wait? Are you able to learn?
Is getting an answer your only concern?
Can anything hide your impatience that burns
from a God who is a consuming fire and knows your heart?

Those who wait on the Lord will indeed find great strength
Strength that cannot be owned by the proud, but the meek
It's the joy of the Lord, without which you're weak
Strength by which you can run against a troop and defeat your enemies

Your waiting is precious; your trials are gold
Your tears: liquid praise when the battle gets old
Though the waters rise and the rivers overflow
You're winning! You're winning! You're winning!

Not only so, but we also glory in our sufferings,
because we know that suffering produces perseverance.

ROMANS 5:3 NIV

What promises from God are you waiting to be fulfilled in your life?

GROWING IN...

Persistence

They say you are determined; they say tenacious too
At times they call it stubborn; we both know that it's true!

But it's the force that drives you; that diligent persistence
I'm thankful you don't settle for the path of least resistance!

Keep right on persevering; you dare not give up now
Keep going strong, before too long you'll get to take your bow!

*Pray with unceasing prayer and entreaty on every fitting occasion
in the Spirit, and be always on the alert to seize opportunities
for doing so, with unwearied persistence and entreaty on behalf
of all God's people.*

EPHESIAN 6:18 WEY

Proclaim the message; persist in it whether convenient or not.

2 TIMOTHY 4:2 HCSB

How have you had to learn persistence in your walk with God?
And how have others had to persist with you?

Prayer

Sign me up, I'm joining the ranks
in a war that is fought on the knees
And there I will stay, despite honor or thanks
'til there is no more death or disease

Because I believe He has carried our griefs
plus our sorrow, our sickness and sin
And because up in heaven there are no such thieves
healing must be for us left herein

What if this day each knee, hit its mark, made its plea
would the whole of earth's voice death restrict?
In the peace we cry for, hands would cease from their war
and instead lay themselves on the sick

Enlisted or drafted, you're in, do not shrink!
Let petitions be plenty, not rare
In your eyes, as you rise, see yourself as the link
'cause my friend, we won't win 'cept through prayer

Let distractions lay halt at your feet
'til today's underway; prayers complete

*And in the morning, a long time before daylight, He got up and went out to a
quiet place, and there He gave himself up to prayer.*

Mark 1:35 net

List your current prayer concerns. How can you lay aside distractions so that you can invest concentrated time sitting, listening, and talking to God about these things this week?

Quietness

Tranquility comes
as war surrenders in prayer
The ceasefire begins

Harmony then hums
and I'm no longer ensnared
by sickness or sin

My heart now becomes
quiet and calm and prepared
His peace treaty wins

When He gives quietness, who then can make trouble?

JOB 34:29 NKJV

Yahweh your God is among you, a warrior who saves.
He will rejoice over you with gladness. He will
bring you quietness with His love.

ZEPHANIAH 3:17 HCSB

When is the last time you were quiet for more than five minutes with no distractions? List some strategies for incorporating a quiet time into your daily routine.

Relaxation

Relaxing can be defined
as to rest, chillax and unwind
Take a load off, de-stress
Put your feet up and rest
Or don't, and go out of your mind!

He went out to relax in the field in the early evening.

GENESIS 24:63 NET

No relaxation hath our flesh had,
but on every side we are in tribulation,
without are fightings, within—fears.

2 CORINTHIANS 7:5 YLT

What does relaxation look like to you? How can you keep needed relaxation well-balanced with your work?

Restraint

Restrain my heart within me, Lord
and don't forget my tongue
For though my heart is seasoning
my mouth is very young

And please, oh God, what'er the cost
please make me patient now!
So I can stand, despite demand
beside my every vow

Where there is no revelation, the people cast off restraint.

PROVERBS 29:18 NIV

Don't weary yourself to be rich. In your wisdom, show restraint.

PROVERBS 23:4 WEB

Name a time you had to exercise great restraint.
What was the fruit of that restraint?

Selflessness

Your sacrificial spirit, your altruistic care
you've felt the pain of others, and brought them comfort there

So thoughtful and attentive, benevolent and kind
your touch can heal the hurting; your words can ease the mind

If mercy had a title, and charity, a name
you'd be their special patron in Compassion's Hall of Fame

Defender of the downcast, the guardian of grace
Your selfless smile draws many; it is their hiding place

*We know that our old self was crucified with Him in order
that the body of sin might be brought to nothing,
so that we would no longer be enslaved to sin.*

ROMANS 6:6 ESV

*Do nothing out of selfish ambition or vain conceit.
Rather, in humility value others above yourselves.*

PHILIPPIANS 2:3 NIV

What and when are the greatest areas of temptation for you to be selfish? How can you turn these into opportunities for selflessness?

Self-worth

Check your baggage at the door
if you have ego, drop it
It took ten years to sweep this floor
and seven more to mop it

I wouldn't make you stay outside
and risk a cold or cough
But loud and clear, once you're in here
those shoes are comin' off!

Strength and self-respect are her clothing;
she is facing the future with a smile.

PROVERBS 21:35 BBE

Rather, it should be that of your inner self, the unfading beauty
of a gentle and quiet spirit, which is of great worth in God's sight.

1 PETER 3:4 NIV

At what point in your life have you felt the most worth and with whom?
At what point have you felt the least, and what was the outcome?

Stewardship

I know You hear my prayers for dues and debts
I know you hold provision in Your hand
But if I am to live with no regrets
I want my wealth to enter with a plan
For if I squander riches that You bring
the prayers I prayed were surely prayed in vain
And if I fly my kite without a string
the blessings that You bring will float away
By giving back to others and to You
my stewardship expands and makes You smile
And then, since I no longer muddle through
I'm able to inspire the world in style
And now that wealth has found an open door
the borrower and lender cease to war

And he called him, and said unto him,
How is it that I hear this of thee?
Give an account of thy stewardship;
for thou mayest be no longer steward.

LUKE 16:2 KJV

If you were asked today to give an account of how you have stewarded your resources (financial, relational, talents, etc.) how would you answer? In what way do you desire to be a better steward?

_____

_____

_____

_____

_____

_____

_____

_____

_____

_____

_____

_____

_____

_____

_____

_____

Submission

I've won the Nobel Peace Prize
the twenty-one-gun salute
a Grammy, Tony, Oscar
and a Pulitzer to boot

Olympic medals everywhere
an Eagle Scout badge too
the Heisman and the Winston Cup
with Wimbledon in view

I've won the People's Choice Award
on People magazine
Been decorated by a king
and crowned homecoming queen

My Superbowl ring flashes
like the medals on my chest
But though my trophy case is full
my laurels cannot rest

I still chase after one prize
mere accolades can't bring
With that award: "Submission's Sword"
the victory song I'll sing!

During the days of Jesus' life on earth, He offered up prayers and petitions with fervent cries and tears to the one who could save him from death, and He was heard because of His reverent submission.

HEBREWS 5:7 NIV

Who, besides God, do you submit to in your life?
Would God say you are exhibiting "reverent submission"?

Tact

Lips be thoughtful, mouth be wise
Tongue be fully circumcised
Words be whittled with a knife
Censor all that is not life

Hand be ready to move in
Cover death from nose to chin
Mouth be moistened, smile don't frown!
Blessings flow where curses drown

Daniel spoke to him with wisdom and tact.

DANIEL 2:14 NIV

Would you consider yourself a tactful person?
Give an example of when you gracefully handled a delicate situation.

Teamwork

We all believe in teamwork
and need a helping hand
But hesitate to collaborate
and remain a one-man band

We want to feel the limelight
take credit and a bow
We think that if we take some help
it undermines the "wow"

But some jobs take a village
Some burdens need a group
And never was a battle won
without an allied troop

The common good still needs us
to set a common goal
Then common sense will lead us
if we'll give up control

Let's put our heads together
Join forces 'til it's done
And let good ol' team spirit
make all our hard work fun

Therefore we ought to support such people, so that we become coworkers in cooperation with the truth.

3 JOHN 1:8 NET

How are you at working with others?
How could you improve your cooperation and collaboration skills?

Trust

Why on earth should I come under?
Yield, and let them steal my thunder?
They've no right to take my plunder
just to make themselves rotunder
If I trust them but they blunder
will my world be torn asunder?
Or will God, the great refunder
See my faith, and bless? I wonder…

Let not your hearts be troubled. Trust in God: trust in me also.

JOHN 14:1 WEY

How has broken trust affected others' ability to trust in you and your ability to trust in others? How do you want to grow in trust (you trusting others and others trusting you)?

Truth

Principles and decency
with scrupulous sincerity
is what God longs to see in me and mine
If I can teach, but not condemn
and plant truth deep inside of them
then we would be a priceless gem and shine

The world is dark with fraud and lies
The truths of God have been revised
and decency is now despised throughout
But if we'll value righteousness
good character and faithfulness
we'll rid the world of crookedness, no doubt

And if our ethics can survive
and honesty will come alive
trustworthiness can be revived and show
Then trust will have a fighting a chance
fidelity and real romance
and truth can finally take a stance and grow

*Jesus answered, "You say that I am a king. In fact, the reason
I was born and came into the world is to testify to the truth.
Everyone on the side of truth listens to me."*

JOHN 18:37 NIV

What evidence do you see that the world is turning its back on absolute truth? Examine your own life and ask the Spirit of Truth (the Holy Spirit) to give you a love for truth.

GROWING IN...
Understanding

It's the age-old question
we all have asked
at some point in our praying past

Why are some healed
and others, no?
Why do some stay, while others go?

We're told to pray
We're told to fast
We're told to seek and knock and ask

We build our faith
and learn our lines
and hope for miracles and signs

Then sickness comes
and there you are
with illness, pain, a surgeon's scar

But hear me out
and please don't judge
'cause I'd like to give our faith a nudge

The Word can heal
There's power within!
Each denomination has its spin

Job was healed
Paul? Not sure
But the Bible says ask God to cure

But when delayed
or worse, declined
a thousands thoughts race through your mind

Was it his faith?
Was it her sin?
Did she just throw the towel in?

Was it territorial?
Or was it worse?
He forgot a generational curse!

Should I change views?
Should I change pews?
Should I just live my life confused?

Should I lay down?
Should I move on?
Please help me, God. My faith is gone

It's hard, I know
We've all been there
But doubt and faith, the stage won't share

If you lose faith now
If you change your stance
Will healing ever have a chance?

It's best to ask
It's best to believe!
Don't plan to ache. Don't plan to grieve

Lazarus would say,
"Give death a black eye."
Solomon would say, "There's a time to die."

And when you meet Job
he'll be talkin' to Paul
They'll be talking 'bout timing, and life's curtain call

You'll see all your loved ones
They'll fill in the gaps
Things you couldn't see here when you had to play taps

There's a time to laugh
There's a time to cry
There's a time to be born and a time to die

Keep going! Keep praying!
Don't dare give up now!
You made God a promise! He made you a vow!

You're going to live forever!
Though not here, my friend
But you win no matter how life finds its end

Your faith is too strong for doubt to destroy
So give God your grief
He'll give you His joy

Trust in the LORD with all your heart
And do not lean on your own understanding.

PROVERBS 3:5 NASB

What are some trails the Lord has allowed you to walk through in life that you just did not understand? What has been the outcome that journey?

_____

_____

_____

_____

_____

_____

_____

_____

_____

_____

_____

_____

_____

_____

_____

_____

_____

_____

_____

Uniqueness

Roses are red and violets, blue
People, like flowers, are each different too
Some are deliberate and others less hurried,
Some tend to dream while others just worry

Some are affectionate, others reserved
Some have great fear, and others, great nerve
Some folks are driven; others content
Some can take jokes but cannot take a hint

Some are tenacious, others are frail
Some cannot win while others can't fail
Whatever we are, we are by God's hand
And whatever we're not, we become as we stand

Do opposites attract? Or do they offend?
Do we all become one as we each become friends?
This one thing I know, as I've traveled this far:
whatever I'm not, I know that you are

When I feel forgotten and life takes a toll
you add yourself to me and make me feel whole
I treasure our contrasts, our likenesses too
But come what may, know that I do treasure you

But He is unique and who can turn Him? And what His soul desires, that He does.

JOB 23:13 NASB

Name four things about yourself that are unique to you.
Ask God why He made you that way and what He wants you
to accomplish in the earth with those traits.

Unity

The time is now; the clock has chimed
The seed is good; the soil is primed
We're woven together, like the words of this rhyme
independently important, but inseparable

Our land has woes, but that won't last
We look to the future and pray o'er the past
We run, we leap, we pray, we fast
and the strongholds of heaven come down

From Montana's mountains to Florida's coasts
from Virginia's valleys to the hills Vermont boasts
the prayer of the saints and the heavenly hosts
is, "God shed His grace on thee"

From New Mexico deserts to Hawaii's cool rains
from Illinois flatlands to Indiana's plains
from the lowlands of Texas to the highlands of Maine
we are one nation under God

There's a river of fruitfulness this land does secrete
making Idaho's potatoes and Iowa's corn sweet
giving Georgia its peaches and Kansas its wheat
to remind us we're called to feed the nations

With New Hampshire's granite and West Virginia's coal
North Carolina's silver and Nevada's gold
from the minerals of Ohio to Oklahoma's oil
we're full of hidden treasures!

On New Jersey's gardens and Minnesota's pines
in Nebraska's farmlands and Maryland's mines
on Connecticut's oaks and California's vines
grow the fruit of bounty and abundance

With Wisconsin's dairies and Delaware's blue hens
Kentucky's horses and South Carolina's wrens
with Pennsylvania's chocolate and Alabama's shrimp
this is indeed a land of milk and honey!

From New York's harbor to Massachusetts' bays
Mississippi's river "Pearl" to Michigan's Great Lakes
from Utah's Great Salt Lake to Rhode Island's "Ocean State"
we flow together with a living water

From Arizona's canyon to the Colorado peaks
from Arkansas' great healing springs and restful fishing creeks
to Washington, DC, where freedom rings and people speak
this land is your land; this land is mine

From the deep plains and prairies, rise Missouri's high plateaus
like the hills of Tennessee with its valleys, highs and lows
in the North Dakota badlands blooms the wild prairie rose
proving we're called to unity with diversity

With Oregon's Blue Mountains and Wyoming's Yellowstone Lake
from South Dakota's Black Hills to Alaska's white snowflakes
with Louisiana's river "Red" and Washington: "The Evergreen State"
we definitely bear a coat of many colors!

United we will stand and divided we will fall
We must each one guard his liberty and justice for all
From east to west and north to south, we're family, great and small
For a house divided against itself won't stand

We're linked by more than government, by more than just state lines
We're bound by more than documents democracy designed
We're members of one body, different functions intertwined
How beautiful it is when brethren dwell together in unity!

Oh say, can you see? We are family with one name!
May God be our footing; may love be our aim
It's our power, our passion! It's how we became
The United States of America

Through the peace that ties you together,
do your best to maintain the unity that the Spirit gives.

EPHESIANS 4:3 GW

In what areas of your life does the enemy seem to come against your unity with others? How can you be wise to those divisions and avoid disunity?

_____

_____

_____

_____

_____

_____

_____

_____

_____

_____

_____

_____

_____

_____

_____

_____

_____

Virtue

Today, oh God, I vow to put my heart into Your hands
and humbly plead for You to knead it 'til it understands

That words alone cannot fulfill the duties that are mine
But virtue too, toward man and You, is what I must combine

So give me eyes to see my face and ears to hear my words
That I might judge myself as pure so I can rest assured

Amen

*For this very reason make every effort
to supplement your faith with virtue.*

2 PETER 1:5 RSV

*Who may make discovery of a woman of virtue?
For her price is much higher than jewels.*

PROVERBS 31:10 BBE

Do you have a love for virtue?

What does God want virtue to look like in your own life?

Wisdom

This year you were given some chances
31 million in fact
To alter your own circumstances
to better them, to be exact

Some days you did better than others
Some days you fell flat on your face
Some days you'd not trade for another
Most days you were thankful for grace

Each second you had was a gift, though
Each second that came and then went
It hoped it would be met with courage
It hoped it would be wisely spent

31 million seconds now leave you
31 million more on their way
What will you wisely choose to accomplish
with your 86,000 today?

Walk in wisdom toward those who are outside, redeeming the time.

COLOSSIANS 4:5 KJV

You have countless opportunities every day to be wise. Describe what wisdom feels like as you are exercising it.

Worship

Smooth as chocolate, cool as rain, sweet as honey, an iron-like chain
Essential as light, hot like the wind, as luscious as lather on red raw skin

A rock and a diamond, a whispering knife
Beneath His breast, the milk of life

A symphony of love, in storm, death or flood
His music, white worship that runs through my blood

One vision for always to sing and to scream
A thousand bare petals, we garden and dream

In summer, in winter, the sun and the moon
Eternity shines, not a moment too soon

True juice crushed from beauty, a spring from above
I'm all I can be, when drunk in His love

God is spirit, and those who worship Him
must worship in spirit and truth.

JOHN 4:24 RSV

How can you be more of a participant in worship and less of a spectator?

" 𝒳 "

X marks the spot
and soldiers take aim
The target's in reach once you give it a name

And when you are lost
destination unclear
an X on a map gives a calm "you are here"

Of course, then there's math
equations and sums
and X is the answer you're happy that comes

So, likewise in life
and in this bold book
you've ciphered some problems your heart once forsook

You've mapped out a course
You've aimed high for growth
You've targeted breakthrough and taken an oath

Mark X on your spots
then fill in your blanks
and when that growth comes, give God all the thanks!

I press toward the mark for the prize of the high calling of God in Christ Jesus.

Philippians 3:14 kjv

What are the main areas of growth in your life that
this devotional journal has shed light on for you?

_____

_____

_____

_____

_____

_____

_____

_____

_____

_____

_____

_____

_____

_____

_____

_____

_____

_____

_____

Yearning

I yearn for breakthrough

Like the night yearns for daybreak
like the ocean yearns to wave its hand and touch a stable plain
like the mountaintop yearns for daring feet
and the sun's rays long to part the clouds

I yearn

Like the deathbed yearns for second chances
and the unheld hand yearns for love
like the barren field yearns for seed
and the empty womb yearns for life

I yearn

Like the deafened ear yearns for sound
And the muted tongue yearns to sing
Like the unprayed prayer yearns to rise
And the continual prayer yearns to rest

I yearn

My soul yearns, even faints, for the courts of the LORD;
my heart and my flesh cry out for the living God.

PSALM 84:2 NIV

For what do you yearn?

GROWING IN...

Zeal

Passion and fervor
are restless observers
and always impatient to share
They're hard to explain
cannot be contained
and you don't have to ask if they're there

In every instance
the cure for indifference
they ponder and poke and they prod
They work 'til they drop
don't know when to stop
especially when it's for God

But what if this zeal
we all sometimes feel
could be bottled and opened on cue?
You'd let out a quip
and take a swift sip
and quickly become the best you

Whatever your need
and regardless of speed
it's zeal that will pick up the pace
From boldness to prayer
to truth (if you dare)
drink long for the whole human race

Your gusto to grow
and to never plateau
will change everything but your name
Your heart's disposition
and character's mission
will set your whole spirit aflame

So burn like a fire!
Intense, even higher!
Your life is God's gift to His earth!
Burn strong, grow in grace
put faith on your face
then watch and you'll learn what you're worth

Never be lacking in zeal, but keep your spiritual fervor, serving the Lord.

ROMANS 12:11 NIV

Glance back throughout your journaling. How has your zeal for the Lord
and for growth increased in the areas this journal addresses?

About the Author

Laura Harris Smith lives in Nashville, Tennessee, where she and her husband, Chris, pastor Eastgate Creative Christian Fellowship. Laura is also the founder and director of the Eastgate Creative Arts Conservatory, where she mentors young writers from all over the world in her online writing courses (visit www.LauraHarrisSmith.com/Online_Writing_Class.html).

"I enjoy all genres of writing, but to be honest, I often hear in rhyme. Grocery lists, conversations, even prayers on occasion," says Laura. "In third grade I decided to write a light-hearted poem about Watergate—don't ask me why—and then I entered it into a 4-H poetry contest at school and won third place. I can't say my fellow seven-year-olds could fully comprehend the topic as I read my poem aloud that day, but then, neither could I. That's the beauty of poetry though. A seven-year-old can take a national crisis and with just a few rhymes, divert everyone's attention with an unsophisticated perspective that results in a happier outlook."

Laura is the author of numerous books, including *Seeing the Voice of God: What God is Telling You Through Dreams and Visions* (Chosen Books, 2014), which topped the charts at #1 on the Amazon Best Sellers List in several Christian categories. She speaks and ministers nationally and internationally across denominational lines and is known for bringing a light-hearted look to the heaviest of biblical topics. Her presentations always include her entertaining poetry.

Married for over thirty years, Chris and Laura have six children: Jessica, Julian, Jhason, Jeorgi, Jude, and Jenesis, all home schooled and all creative in their own right. With half of them now grown and married, they also have a growing list of grandchildren that outnumbers the kids.

Invite Laura to speak at

booking@LauraHarrisSmith.com

Learn more about Laura's ministry at

www.LauraHarrisSmith.com

www.EastgateCCF.com

Rhyme Schemes

Affirmation – ABB tercet

Boldness – AA couplet

Charity – ABCB quatrain

Commitment – AA couplet

Consecration – AAAA monorhyme quatrain

Contentment – AABCCB sestet

Courtesy – ABCB quatrain

Creativity – AABCCB sestet

Deliverance – sonnet ABABCDCDEFEFGG

Dependence – AAAAAAAA
                    monorhyme octaves

Discernment – AA couplet

Discipline – ABAB quatrain

Discretion – AA couplet

Enduranace – ABCCB quintain

Excellence – AA heroic couplet
                (iambic pentameter)

Faith – ABCB quatrain

Fearlessness – AA couplet / sonnetina due

Flexibility – AABCCB sestet

Forgiveness – AA couplet

Friendship – AABB sonnetina tre

Generosity – ABB rondel

Gentleness – a rhyming haiku, ABC

Gratitude – AA couplet

Health – ABCB quatrain

Honor – AA couplet

Hope – ABAB quatrain

Humility – AAAB quatrain

Identity – iambic tetrameter quatrains

Influence – ABCB quatrain

Intimacy – sonnet ABABCDCDEFEFGG

Joy – AAB tercet

Kindness – ABAB quatrain

Leadership – iambic tetrameter

Love – AA couplet

Loyalty – ABB tercet

Maturity – limerick

Mercy – AABB quatrain

Nutrition – AAAAAAAA monorhyme octaves

Obedience – ABCB quatrain

Patience – AA couplet

Peace – AABB quatrain

Perseverence – AAAB quatrain

Persistence – AA couplet

Prayer – ABAB heroic sonnet

Quietness – a rhyming haiku, ABC

Relaxation – limerick

Restraint – ABCB quatrain

Selflessness – AA couplet

Self-worth – ABAB auatrain

Stewardship – sonnet ABABCDCDEFEFGG

Submission – ABCB quatrain

Tact – AABB quatrain

Teamwork – ABCB quatrain

Trust – AAAAAAAA monorhyme octave

Truth – AABCCB sestet

Understanding – ABB tercet

Uniqueness – AABB quatrain

Unity – AAAB quatrain

Virtue – AA couplet

Wisdom – ABAB quatrain

Worship – AA couplet

"X" – ABB tercet

Yearning – ABCD lament

Zeal – AABCCB sestet